We are Different,
You and I

Helen Iles

National Library of Australia Cataloguing-in-Publication entry

Creator: Iles, Helen, 1954- author, book designer.

Title: We are different, you and I / Helen Iles ; graphic designer Helen Iles.

ISBN: 9781876922313 (paperback)

Target Audience: For pre-school age.

Subjects: Cultural awareness--Juvenile fiction. Toleration--Juvenile fiction.

Dewey Number: A823.4

Published by:

Linellen Press / Teddy Books Imprint

265 Boomerang Road

Oldbury Western Australia 6121

ACKNOWLEDGMENTS

My first thank you goes to the unknown makers of these wonderful teddy bears, Charlie, Mikey, Tatty and Woofus, all collected from a huge cardboard box at Coles stores across the State, all sadly missing their tags. Grump-pa was found loitering in an Opportunity Shop in Kalgoorlie, Western Australia, while Sam was my sister's kind replacement when I lost my beloved Rottweiler. I thank each supplier of these delightful comforts to the soul. They will live happily ever after in my care.

I also thank dear, sweet Fairy Princess Sara (great-granddaughter Sierra) for tolerating the various photo-shoots at such a young age. May this book, when she can read, teach her tolerance and acceptance of all those around her.

My sincerest thanks to June Earle, my good friend and skilled photographer, for her creative thought and talent throughout the visual aspects of this production. Her gift with the camera has brought my friends to life.

We are Different, You and I

Tatty Teddy sat at the table with his eyes down and his ears falling flat. He felt very unhappy as the other teddies laughed at him.

"You look so tatty," Charlie, the newest teddy, had said. "Your fur is all over the place while my fur is so neat and soft."

All the teddies looked at Tatty's coat, which was indeed rough and ragged.

"And you Grump-pa Bear," Charlie added, "you are so so small."

Then Grump-pa Bear looked sad, and his eyes and head dropped down.

Fairy Princess Sara patted Tatty, and she kissed poor Grump-pa Bear and poured them both a cup of cold, white milk.

"Be nice, Charlie Bear. We are all so different – every one of us," she said.

"Look at you and Woofus. You are BROWN and Woofus is WHITE."

White

Black

"Look at Woofus and Sam. Woofus is WHITE and Sam is BLACK."

"Look at Grump-pa Bear and Tatty. Both are very old, but Grump-pa is SMALL and Tatty is very BIG.

"Look at you and Woofus and Sam. You are all Teddy Dogs."

"And look at Tatty and Grump-pa Bear. They are
Teddy Bears."

"And look at Mikey – he is not like any of you at all."

"Now look at Sam and Mikey. Sam is so very serious while Mikey is such a monkey."

"And look at me ... I am not like any of you either. But we are all very special, Charlie."

"Grump-pa Bear is special because he is so small I can carry him with me when there is no room to take all of you."

"Woofus is special because he is white and lights up my room at night so I can see."

Mikey is special because he always makes me laugh.

"Sam is special because he is strong and sits by my bed at night and keeps me safe."

"Tatty is special because he is made from my Nannie's favourite coat and I remember her every time I hug him."

She gave Tatty a great big hug right then and Tatty lifted his big brown head and smiled.

"So you see, Charlie Dog, we are all very different but all so very special and I love all of you just the same."

Charlie's head began to droop.

"And you, Charlie Teddy Dog, are very special because you are our newest friend and we can teach you how special it is to be nice and always say nice things."

Fairy Princess Sara smiled and winked at all her friends

and all her special Teddy friends winked back.

***

ABOUT THE AUTHOR

West Australian author Helen Iles is a grandmother and great grandmother. Her children's books aim to teach children social values and life lessons using magical realism, and are also available as enriched e-books to allow young readers an audio-visual reading experience. A novelist and poet, animator and editor, Helen teaches creative writing and guides new writers towards publication. Her other interests include training and caring for horses, graphic design, writing adult novels and travelling overseas.

www.ingramcontent.com/pod-product-compliance
Lightning Source LLC
Chambersburg PA
CBHW042108040426
42448CB00002B/180